Teen Speak

Parent Workbook

Introduction

Foreword

Every parent is the expert when it comes to their teen, although we know teens are unique and respond differently to the ways we talk with them. This workbook is meant to provide you with some new strategies for the ups and downs of parenting teens. It is important to have many strategies in our "hip pocket" to connect with teens, particularly when we talk with them about risky behaviors and situations they may experience.

Just as teens are unique – so are parents. Throughout this workbook we've included a variety of thought-provoking questions, role-play scenarios, and quizzes, to help you think through your personal beliefs and how they may affect your interactions or communication with your teen. These activities will also help you identify the strategies that feel most comfortable and may work best for you. Some of the exercises in this workbook may not be the exact right fit for your communication style. We encourage you to try all of the exercises, even the ones that might feel a little bit out of your comfort zone – it can remind us that teens often feel out of their own comfort zone too!

This workbook was designed to give you the opportunity to dig deeper into the strategies outlined in my book Teen Speak: A how to guide for real talks with teens about sex, drugs and other risky behaviors and in the Teen Speak online learning modules. The chapters in this workbook correspond to the chapters in Teen Speak. This workbook should be used to enhance your understanding and use of the skills as you read through the book or work through the online learning modules. The best way to use this workbook is to read each chapter in Teen Speak and/or complete an online learning module, then work your way through the corresponding chapter in this workbook.

More information about *Teen Speak* and the online modules can be found at: PossibilitiesforChange.com/TeenSpeak

1

Foundations For Talking
With Your Teen

PARENT PERSPECTIVE: How would you describe your relationship with your teen? Do you feel they are honest about risky situations they have experienced or heard about?

_____

_____

_____

Reminder: The causes of death in 3 out of every 4 teens are due to risky behaviors.

QUICK QUIZ #1: List 3 common risky behaviors that contribute to teen deaths.

1. _____

2. _____

3. _____

What if your teen is engaging in risky behaviors? Think about the range of risk behaviors your teen might be experimenting with. How do you feel about these behaviors? How do your personal or religious beliefs influence your ability to discuss them with your teen?

_____

_____

_____

_____

REFLECTION: Imagine your teen tells you they are actively engaging in risky behaviors.

- What would your immediate or "knee-jerk" reaction be to hearing that news?

  _____

- Are you willing to engage in a two-way discussion with your teen on this topic even if it goes against your personal beliefs?

  _____

- What are some strategies that you can prepare in advance that will help you stay "cool" or calm during your discussion (silently counting to 5, repeating what your teen has said before responding, or something else…)?

  _____

Reminder: Studies show that having a strong relationship with your teen is one of the biggest positive influences on their behavior.

2

Teen Development –
The Good, the Bad and the Beautiful

PARENT PERSPECTIVE: What changes (physically, emotionally, and cognitively) have you noticed in your teen?

_____

_____

_____

Reminder: At no other time (except in their first two years of life) do our sons and daughters go through so much growth and change, so quickly.

QUICK QUIZ #2: What are the four stages of development that teens will experience during puberty?

1. _____   3. _____

2. _____   4. _____

REFLECTION: It's natural to expect a teen to respond to challenges with the same reasoning, logic, or approach that you would. Think through some conversations you've had with your teen that have caused conflict or frustration between the two of you. Looking back, how could their stages of development have played a role in your discussion?

_____

_____

_____

_____

Reminder: All of these rapid changes may seem as if there is something drastically wrong with your teen, but they are completely normal.

3

Physical Development – Body Changes

PARENT PERSPECTIVE: How have your teen's physical changes impacted their behaviors and feelings? Have you heard any comments from them about their appearance or how their body feels?

_____

_____

_____

_____

_____

Reminder: Teens who physically mature earlier appear older, and they're often treated as if they are more socially and emotionally mature, even though this often isn't true.

QUICK QUIZ #3: What are some things to watch out for as your teen develops physically?

1. _____

2. _____

3. _____

4. _____

> **Reminder:** Take your teen's comments about their appearance seriously and spend time <u>listening</u> (without jumping in and talking).

SKILLS: Here are 3 steps you can use when discussing physical changes with your teen:

- Step 1: Acknowledge your teen's feelings and what they are saying.

- Step 2: Allow them time to respond. Try not to lecture.

- Step 3: Provide a different view of the situation and help your teen problem solve whenever possible .

PRACTICE: Try these 3 steps during your next car ride or texting conversation with your teen.

Example

You hear screaming and something hit your daughter's bedroom door. You notice her jeans on the floor and realize she was trying to put on jeans that she has outgrown.

- **Step 1:** Start by acknowledging her feelings, "You are upset about not fitting into your favorite jeans."
- **Step 2:** Allow her time to respond, "Yes, I'm so fat right now! I hate myself!"

  Acknowledge what you are hearing, "You are going through a hard time right now. Your body is growing really fast and your clothes can't grow with it"

  Allow her time to respond. Don't be uncomfortable with silence, "I wish I would just stop growing"
- **Step 3:** Provide a different view of the situation and a possible solution, "Changing sizes is a normal part of growing up. What if we go out this weekend and buy you a few things to fit the 'new you'?"

Reminder: You will be tempted to tell them things like, "You don't have to look like everyone else. You are perfect just as you are. The people you see on TV and in magazines aren't normal." These may be true statements – but not necessarily what they need to encourage healthy physical development.

4

Cognitive Development – Thinking Skills

PARENT PERSPECTIVE: What changes have you noticed in the way your child thinks since becoming a teen? How have conversations with them changed – do you find him or her to be more argumentative, quieter or more introspective, a mix of these?

_____

_____

_____

_____

These are normal behaviors teens display:
1. Arguing for the state of arguing.
2. Jumping to conclusions.
3. Being self-centered.
4. Constantly finding fault in your position.
5. Being overly dramatic.

When you experience these behaviors from your teen, they can cause you to instantly react. How will you take a "step back" and apply some of the strategies discussed in chapter 4?

1. First take a mental pause. Ask yourself, is this worth arguing about or can I let it go?

2. Set ground rules for a healthy debate (at a time when you are not arguing). What are some of the rules that might work for you and your teen?

_____

_____

One idea is to take turns sharing thoughts one at a time. When one person is talking, the other listens – then you switch.

3. Think through how you might start the conversation about ground rules. Try saying it out loud and/or role play it with a friend or family member until it feels comfortable and easy to remember.

Use an "opener" to get the ground rules discussion started:

"We have been arguing a lot lately and I don't want that to affect our relationship. I would like us to set some 'rules' to follow whenever we start disagreeing about something. Are you OK with this?"

Reminder: As teens mature, their decision making skills increase, but in stressful situations they often revert back to the concrete thinking of early development.

REFLECTION: Think about how your teen reacts to stressful situations and how you react to stressful situations? Are there similarities or differences?

_____

_____

_____

_____

_____

_____

_____

Reminder: The more you stay calm, be directive in your conversations, and role model good communication, the more likely your teen will be able to navigate their changing thoughts and emotions to develop into successful young adults.

5

Emotional Development – Feelings

PARENT PERSPECTIVE: What emotional changes have you noticed in your teen? Have there been extreme changes or a lack of emotions?

_____

_____

_____

_____

Reminder: One of the most significant changes in emotional development in teens is the shift from the world revolving around family to revolving around friends.

The 4 areas of emotional development include:

1. Self-awareness
2. Social-awareness
3. Self-management
4. Establishing healthy, rewarding relationships

WARNING SIGNS DURING ADOLESCENCE

1. Fear and withdrawal
2. Too much focus or concern about their bodies
3. Changes in eating or irregular meal patterns (like skipping breakfast or dieting)
4. Losing sleep or trouble sleeping
5. Ups and downs of social relationships that never seem to end

Reminder: Increasing independence, close ties to people outside the family, and the developing need and capacity for intimacy – are all normal and important indicators of teen development. These are important steps in the journey to developing healthy adult relationships with others AND with you!

REFLECTION: Think through the ways you stay connected with your teen. As their interests are changing and evolving some of these opportunities may evolve too:

- Family dinners
- One-on-one outings (to the mall, a walk, or even a weekly grocery trip together)
- A weekend family only getaway
- Movie night
- Drive time

What are some ways you can stay connected with your teen that would work for you and your family's routine?

_____

_____

Reminder: While friends have a big influence on teens' day-to-day identity choices, research shows that having family members who teens feel connected to is even more important during adolescence than at any other time.

6

Sexual Development – Changing Desires

PARENT PERSPECTIVE: What concerns or thoughts do you have about your teens sexual development? What types of conversations have you had about sex with your teen? Think about your personal beliefs or experiences– how might those influence your discussions?

_____

_____

_____

_____

_____

Reminder: Talking with, not at, your teen about sex is very important. Teens' decisions about engaging in sexual activity are not our decisions, unless we are connected to their hip 24/7.

You are a role model for your son or daughter. If you engage in an authentic, respectful two-way discussion with your teen about sex — they are more likely to hear your views and opinions and act on them.

QUICK QUIZ #4: What are the 6 influencers on a teen's decisions about sex?

1. _____

2. _____

3. _____

4. _____

5. _____

6. _____

REFLECTION: How will you guide your teen toward healthy sexual decisions? Think about how you might use some of these strategies:

Encourage your teen to love and value themselves.

- What are some phrases you can use to encourage your teen?

_____

Encourage your teen to leave nice at the door, girls in particular.

- What ways can you empower your teen to take into account their own desires when making sexual decisions?

_____

Clearly express your expectations for their sexual behaviors and provide guidance, not directives.

- What are your expectations for your teens sexual behaviors?

_____

7

Teens and Risky Behaviors – What Are They Doing?

PARENT PERSPECTIVE: What behaviors are you most concerned about with your teen and why?

_____

_____

_____

Reminder: A teens most serious health issues are not caused by disease, but instead result from behaviors, experiences, and feelings.

QUICK QUIZ #5: What is the first and most important step in reducing your teen's risk?

_____

_____

_____

Reminder: Managing your emotions and reactions (facial expressions, language) is critical to having a discussion that leads your teen towards choosing safer options rather than riskier behaviors.

ROLE PLAY: Try practicing a conversation with a partner or friend about a risky behavior before having it with your teen.

REFLECTION: What is a risky situation you want to help your teen plan for?

_____

_____

The following questions may help prepare you for the discussion:

1. How can you empathize with your teen on how difficult their decision might be?

   _____

   _____

2. What are the pros and cons of each choice?

   _____

   _____

3. What are some possible solutions to help your teen make a safe and healthy decision?

   _____

   _____

Reminder: Studies show that if teens think through and plan for future risky situations they are more likely to make safer decisions.

8

Changing Behaviors

PARENT PERSPECTIVE: Changing a behavior (or going against a friend's behavior) is extremely difficult. Think about a behavior you have changed. What motivated or helped you the most?

_____

_____

_____

> **Reminder:** Knowledge (what teens know about the potential consequences of a behavior) has shown to have very little effect on whether or not a teen decides to participate in risky behaviors.

QUICK QUIZ #6: What are 2 factors that play the biggest role in your teens decision making?

    1. _____   2. _____

Reminder: Planning is key. A teen is more likely to follow through with a decision about being safe when faced with a risky situation when they have thought through the steps they will need to take.

PRACTICE: The guide below can help you plan with your teen. Try it using this situation: *Your son or daughter has previously made the decision to not drink alcohol and you have learned their friends are drinking on the weekends.*

1. Start with an empathetic statement that includes a reminder of their planned behavior. In your own words, how would you start the conversation?

    _____

    _____

2. Let them respond and allow a few seconds for silence. Think about how your teen might respond.

3. Use a follow-up question to ask what they think they can do to make sure they are not peer pressured. What question would you use?

    _____

    _____

4. LISTEN to what they say and validate them. Think about how your teen might respond.

    _____

    _____

5. Ask permission to offer suggestions. Using your own words, how would you ask permission?

    _____

    _____

6. Give several suggestions to avoid drinking with friends. What suggestions can you think of?

_____

_____

Example of practicing planning with your teen around sex:

1. Empathize: "It can be hard to wait to have sex when you are in a relationship and I know you are committed to doing that."

2. Let them respond, then follow up with a question like "What do you feel you need in order to keep this commitment to yourself?"

3. Listen to what they say, validate, then ask permission "Those are good ideas. Can I share some more things for you to think about?"

4. Provide suggestions for them to consider like avoiding being alone in a house with their partner.

QUICK QUIZ #7: What is the greatest indicator that a teen will be successful in changing their behavior or in making safer choices?

_____

_____

9

Strengths of Teens – They Are Amazing!

PARENT PERSPECTIVE: Many parents feel that a strengths-based approach (vs. a "warning" approach) is too soft or not-effective. What are your feelings about a strengths-based parenting style?

_____

_____

_____

What gifts, talents, and skills make your teen special?

_____

_____

_____

Reminder: Part of a parents' job is to make sure our daughters and sons recognize their strengths and build on them.

Teens live up or down to our expectations. List 3 expectations you have for your teen.

1. _____

2. _____

3. _____

Be mindful of opportunities to identify and reflect strengths during your daily interactions, not just when having discussions about risky behaviors. Don't forget about your strengths as well. Using the circle of courage framework below, under each of the 4 essential areas list yours and your teens strengths:

- BELONGING:

  _____

  _____

- MASTERY:

  _____

  _____

- INDEPENDENCE:

  _____

  _____

- GENEROSITY:

  _____

  _____

10

Proven Communication Strategies – Setting the Stage

PARENT PERSPECTIVE: Adopting a new communication style isn't easy - it's a behavior change after all! To help you make and sustain this change in your own behavior, it can help to apply the strategies in this chapter: What are your...

1. Reasons and motivation for wanting to communicate more effectively with your teen?

   _____

   _____

2. What might get in the way of trying new communication strategies?

   _____

   _____

3. What could you do to overcome these barriers and successfully use some new strategies?

   _____

   _____

As you know, teens act on impulse and rarely think through the pros and cons of their decisions. Below list possible pros and cons your teen may have for engaging in each behavior. For this exercise it is important that you look at things from your teenager's point of view – not from the point of view of a parent.

Behavior	Pros	Cons
Unprotected Sex	_____ _____	_____ _____
Texting and Driving	_____ _____	_____ _____
(Insert Your Own Behavior)	_____ _____	_____ _____

If a teen is very resistant to changing unsafe behaviors, your rules and punishments may come into play. What consequences would you give your teen if they refused to change the following behaviors?

- Unprotected Sex

  _____

- Texting and Driving

  _____

- (Insert Your Own Behavior)

  _____

REFLECTION: How would you discuss these consequences with your teen? Here's an example of using a reflection statement to explain the connection of risk behaviors and consequences with your teen:

It is so important for you to text while driving that you are OK with (insert your punishment).

11

Building a Strong Foundation

PARENT PERSPECTIVE: What things have you done to build a strong foundation for communicating with your teen? What has worked well? What hasn't worked well?

_____

_____

_____

_____

The 4 strategies for building a strong foundation for communication with your teen include:
1. Asking Permission
2. Giving Information Simply
3. Offering Concern
4. Giving a Menu of Options

For some parents asking permission can feel like you are giving up your authority or "caving in" to your teen. Think about your own interactions with a supervisor or boss. Do you think any less of a supervisor who asks you questions like "When would be a good time to talk about...", or when a supervisor expresses concern about you, or gives you permission to disagree with them? Probably not! These strategies build respect between you and your teen – increasing the chances they will hear what you have to say and come to you more often for advice.

QUICK QUIZ #8: Building a strong foundation starts with ASKING PERMISSION. What are 2 benefits to asking your teen permission, before jumping into a discussion with them?

1. _____

2. _____

PRACTICE: ASKING PERMISSION. Let's say you want to talk to your teen about their friends. You could ask permission like: *"Can we talk about Jamie?"*

What are 2 more ways you could ask permission to talk to your teen about their friends?

_____

_____

What are some ways to respond if your teen says "no"?

_____

_____

Reminder: When teens are given the opportunity to say 'yes' before you start talking, they pay more attention to what you are saying.

QUICK QUIZ #9: Building a strong foundation continues with how we GIVE INFORMATION. What are 3 key things to remember when giving information to teens?

1. _____

2. _____

3. _____

> **Reminder:** Provide information that speaks to your son's or daughter's situation or behavior, something they are actively doing in the here and now – not in the future.

PRACTICE: Building a strong foundation includes OFFERING CONCERN. Give two example statements on how you could offer concern if you found out your teen was in an unhealthy relationship with a friend.

1. _____

   _____

2. _____

   _____

> **Reminder:** Teens feel safe and protected when parents worry about them – as long as they don't feel you are using that to try to control them.

PRACTICE: Building a strong foundation includes providing a MENU OF OPTIONS. When your teen is ready to problem solve or change a behavior, you can offer a menu of options. What are 3 possible options you could offer your teen to avoid unhealthy relationships.

1. _____

2. _____

3. _____

> **Reminder:** Remember, when they choose the option themselves, they are more likely to follow through and act on it.

12

Open-Ended Questions –
Learning More From Your Teen

PARENT PERSPECTIVE: What type of questions do you ask your teen when you want to talk with them about a risky behavior or situation? How does your teen usually respond?

_____

_____

_____

_____

_____

_____

Reminder: Open-ended questions set the tone for communication and allow teens to think through their risky behaviors and possible alternatives.

PRACTICE: OPEN ENDED QUESTIONS are not easily answered with a "yes" or "no". Circle all of the open-ended questions below:

1. Did you have a good day at school?
2. Do you have homework?
3. How important is college to you?
4. Are you hanging out with your friends tomorrow after school?
5. What would it take for you to feel less stressed?
6. When do you see yourself having sex?

QUICK QUIZ #10: What are some of the reasons you shouldn't start a question with "*Why*"?

_____

_____

PRACTICE: FULLY OPEN QUESTIONS can help you learn more from your teen with less questioning by you. Using the fully open question starters below, insert behaviors or situations you would like to discuss with your teen.

- *Tell me about* _____

- *What do you think about* _____

- *How do you decide when to* _____

- *How do you feel about* _____

- *Help me understand* _____

PRACTICE: KEY QUESTIONS move the focus of the discussion to making a change – and ultimately to making a commitment to change or not engage in a risky behavior. What are some examples of key questions you could use with your teen?

_____

_____

_____

_____

Reminder: When you are using key questions, you may be tempted to push for action or argue for change. It is important to remember that the best action at this juncture is to simply listen, then respond with reflection statements.

ROLE PLAY: The best way to get comfortable with using open-ended questions is practice, practice, practice! Start with a partner or friend – ask them about their day or week using only open-ended questions. Dig in and get more details using fully open questions, then if there is a decision to be made, ask a key question.

PRACTICE CHALLENGE: Start small – incorporating open-ended questions into everyday conversations will make it easier and more authentic when you talk about important topics like risky behaviors. To get things started, try going through a whole day without using any "Why?" questions. The results may surprise you!

13

Affirmations –
Focusing on the Positives

PARENT PERSPECTIVE: What are some positive characteristics, achievements and experiences your teen has had? How often do you remind them of these in order to strengthen their self-esteem?

_____

_____

_____

_____

> **Reminder:** Affirmations are not compliments. To be effective affirmations must be genuine and specific and be used to target a strength or support an effort.

AFFIRMATIONS reassure teens that you do not view them as a failure and helps to give them courage to change or avoid risky behaviors – thereby building their:

1. Self-esteem
2. Self-worth

PRACTICE: Using the statement starters below, develop two affirmations for each starter that are specific to your teen.

- *You have....*

  ☐ _____

  ☐ _____

- *You are....*

  ☐ _____

  ☐ _____

- *You feel....*

  ☐ _____

  ☐ _____

- *You believe....*

  ☐ _____

  ☐ _____

Reminder: Affirmations are like salt; a little makes things taste better; a lot makes them hard to swallow.

14

Reflections – Listening and Responding

PARENT PERSPECTIVE: Does your teen feel *heard* when discussing "hot topics" with them? How do you communicate that you are listening?

_____

_____

_____

_____

Reminder: The proper use of reflections can elicit more information sharing from your teen – even more so than open-ended questions.

REFLECTIONS involve:

1. Active listening
2. Stating back what you heard
3. Adding an emphasis, additional meaning, or continuation of thought

The "Sound" of Silence

How comfortable are you with silence? Think of it on a scale of 1-10 where "1" is feeling the need to jump in at the smallest gap in conversation and "10" is being totally comfortable with silence. If your score is anything below 4 you may want to practice with friends and family first.

PRACTICE: Create a response in your own words for each type of reflection below based on this example: *Your teen is struggling to get good grades in school.*

- REPEAT: Repeat back the actual words or repeat an element of what your teen said.
  - *Your reflection :*

  _____

- REPHRASE: Reflect back in your own words the meaning of what they have told you.
  - *Your reflection :*

  _____

- PARAPHRASE: Make a guess at the meaning of what your teen has said.
  - *Your reflection :*

  _____

- REFLECTING FEELING: Confirm your understanding of their feelings.
  - *Your reflection :*

  _____

ROLE PLAY: It can be challenging to control the tone or inflection of your voice. We naturally turn statements into questions without even thinking about it. Ask a partner or friend to make funny, shocking or "far-out" statements to help you practice keeping your tone "neutral" when you respond using a reflection.

> **Reminder:** A good guide is to use 2 to 3 reflections for every question you ask. If you are met with silence, resist the urge to fill the silence immediately with another reflection or question.

15

Change Talk –
Let Them Tell You What
You Want to Hear

PARENT PERSPECTIVE: What are some things your teen has said that lets you know they want to be safe, healthy, productive, or happy?

_____

_____

_____

_____

Reminder: Change Talk is the collective words your teen says that support their interest or intention to make positive changes in their behavior.

QUICK QUIZ #11: What does the acronym DARN stand for related to CHANGE TALK?

D _____   R _____

A _____   N _____

QUICK QUIZ #12: Circle each statement that is CHANGE TALK:

1. I heard the patch can help you stop smoking.
2. I need to wear my seatbelt.
3. I have no issues with my friends.
4. I want to do better in school.
5. I can stop using if I wanted to.

PRACTICE: You can draw out Change Talk from your teen by using open-ended questions.

- EVOCATIVE QUESTION- An open-ended question in which the answer is likely to be change talk.
  - Example: *What could you do to remember to wear your seat belt?*
  - Give an example of an evocative question with another behavior:

  _____

- ENCOURAGE ELABORATION- Ask for more details when a change talk theme emerges.
  - Example: *Help me understand how you are making sure you don't end up at a party where there is drinking?*
  - Give an example of encouraging elaboration with another behavior

  _____

- IMPORTANCE RULER- Assess the importance of the change to your teen or their level of confidence in their ability to change.
  - Example: *On a scale of 1-10, with 10 being '100% absolutely yes' and 1 being 'no, not at all'; how important is it for you to start exercising?"*
  - Give an example of using the importance ruler with another behavior:

  _____

- <u>DECISIONAL BALANCE</u>- Explore the pros and cons of both changing and sustaining a behavior.
  - Example: *What are some reasons for and against breaking up with your boyfriend?*
  - Give an example of using decisional balance with another behavior:

  _____

- <u>QUERYING EXTREMES</u>- Start with your teens current behavior and end with possible negative outcomes of the behavior.
  - Example: *What do you like about texting and driving? What are some of the worst things that could happen?*
  - Give an example of querying extremes with another behavior:

  _____

- <u>LOOKING BACK</u>- Ask about a time before the behavior started.
  - Example: *How much fun were you having with your friends before you got involved with your girlfriend and couldn't hang out with them anymore?*
  - Give an example of looking back with another behavior:

  _____

- <u>LOOKING FORWARD</u>- Ask what may happen if things continue as they are and if they change.
  - Example of things continuing: *What if you stopped taking your medication, what would that look like for you?*
  - Give an example of continuing with another behavior:

  _____

  - Example of things changing: *When you are able to manage your depression, what does that look like? How is your life different?*
  - Give an example of things changing with another behavior:

  _____

> **Reminder:** Change Talk is the collective words your teen says that support their interest or intention to make positive decisions or changes in their behavior.

16

Planning for Success

PARENT PERSPECTIVE: Have you done any planning with your teen around how they will respond when encountering risky situations? What steps have been successful? What steps have they struggled with?

_____

_____

_____

_____

Reminder: If teens haven't thought through how they will respond when faced with a risky situation, they are more likely to allow themselves to be pressured into doing something they didn't intend to do.

SKILL BUILDING: Brainstorming solutions and problem solving is often second-nature for parents. Helping teens learn to brainstorm solutions is important for changing risky behaviors – but it's also an important skill they will use at school, for homework, in a job, etc. Try applying these strategies in your everyday conversations with your teen.

PRACTICE: What open-ended questions can you use to help your teen brainstorm ideas for safer decisions when faced with risky situations?

- _____
- _____
- _____
- _____

Reminder: When your teen does the work needed to develop a safer behavior plan, they are more likely to stick to that plan when encountering risky situations.

BEHAVIOR CHANGE PLAN: Use the following step-by-step guidance to complete a written behavior change plan for a desired change that you have for yourself.

1. **The change I want to make is:** Create a goal describing your behavior change or safer decision.

2. **Three reasons I want to make the change are:** List the reasons for this change.

3. **Some barriers that could get in my way are:** Identify barriers that may get in the way of achieving your goal.

4. **Solutions to overcome these barriers are:** Brainstorm some solutions for the barriers.

5. **Some people who can support me:** Identify the people who will actively support your change process.

6. **The steps I will take to change are:** Describe specific steps needed to achieve the change.

7. **I will know my plan is working if:** Create a measurable goal, this will help you keep track of your progress.

8. **How confident am I that I can make this change:** The last step. Assess your confidence level in achieving the goal.

Worksheet for Change

The change I want to make is...

I want to be active at least 30 minutes for 5 out of 7 days each week.

Some barriers that could get in my way are:

I am tired after school and don't feel like being active. I have a lot of homework and commitments that take up my time.

Three reasons I want to make the change are:

1. Make the basketball team.

2. Look and feel better.

3. Improve my overall health.

Solutions to overcome these barriers are:

1. Take a gym or other fitness class in school.

2. Walk the dog around my neighborhood, before I do anything else after school.

3. Plan activities on the weekend days when I don't have as much going on.

The steps I will take to change are: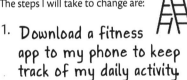

1. Download a fitness app to my phone to keep track of my daily activity

2. Put reminders on my mirror so that I see them every day

3. Tell my mom and dad about my plan so they can support me.

Some people who can support me:

My mom and my dad.

I will know my plan is working if:

If my fitness tracker shows I was active for 20 days at the end of the month.

How confident are you that you can make this change?

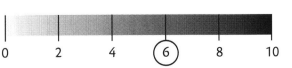

0   2   4   (6)   8   10

Worksheet for Change

The change I want to make is...

Some barriers that could get in my way are:

Three reasons I want to make the change are:

1.

2.

3.

Solutions to overcome these barriers are:

1.

2.

3.

The steps I will take to change are:

1.

2.

3.

Some people who can support me:

I will know my plan is working if:

How confident are you that you can make this change?

0   2   4   6   8   10

17

Handling Difficult Behaviors – Introduction

PARENT PERSPECTIVE: How do you respond when your teen is being difficult? What are you feeling and how does that affect your response?

_____

_____

_____

_____

Reminder: Dealing with difficult behaviors often cause parents to feel a variety of emotions – frustration, anger, anxiety, and despair to name a few.

Common "difficult" teen behaviors include:

1. Arguing
2. Interruptions
3. Denying
4. Ignoring

Reminder: The emotional response when dealing with these difficult behaviors is what causes us to shut down and either avoid meaningful discussions or get into arguments with our teens.

QUICK QUIZ #13: What are the first 2 steps in overcoming difficult behaviors in teens?

Step 1: _____

Step 2: _____

REFLECTION: Think of the last interaction you had with your teen when they were displaying difficult behaviors and answer the self-check questions below.

- Was I dismissing my teen's concerns with statements like *"Your life is not that stressful"*
- Was I acting like the expert and telling my teen all of the consequences of their behavior with comments like *"You need to stop, or XYZ is going to happen to you."*

Reminder: The ultimate goal is to diffuse your teen in order to have a discussion that will lead them toward a positive behavior change and safer decision making."

18 & 19

Handling Difficult Behaviors – Strategies

PARENT PERSPECTIVE: What strategies do you currently use with your teen when they are arguing, ignoring, or interrupting you? What has been effective? What hasn't worked well?

_____

_____

_____

_____

_____

Reminder: Most teens expect adults to respond to them with directives or persuasion, so a reflection often stops them in their tracks.

PRACTICE: Create a reflection for each example of a difficult situation below.

SIMPLE REFLECTION- Repeating what your teen has said to you in a neutral tone.

- **Teen's Statement:** *"I hate going to school every day!"*
- **Your Simple Reflection:**

_____

OMISSION REFLECTION- Reflect the message their behavior is sending.

- **Teen's Behavior:** *Teen is saying nothing while you are trying to talk to them about safe sex. They just keep looking at their phone.*
- **Your Omission Reflection:**

_____

AMPLIFIED REFLECTION- Reflecting what your teen has said in an exaggerated way with empathy and no sarcasm.

- **Teen's Statement:** *"I don't need this stupid depression medication!"*
- **Your Amplified Reflection:**

_____

QUICK QUIZ #14: What does the acronym DEARS stand for related to responding to difficult situations?

D _____

E _____

A _____

R _____

S _____

PRACTICE: Using each DEARS strategy practice creating a response to difficult situations that you have dealt with in your teen.

DEVELOPING DISCREPANCIES – Identifying, and even magnifying, the difference between the teen's stated values or goals and his or her current behaviors.

>> **You can use the phrase** *"On the one hand (name the problem behavior) and on the other hand (identify the goal or dream their behavior may get in the way of)*

Try It Out: Use the phrase above to create a statement you could use to develop a discrepancy between a behavior you notice in your teen that gets in the way of a dream or goal they have.

> **Reminder:** Always end with the dream or goal statement.

Your Statement:

_____

_____

EMPATHIZE – Seeing the world through the eyes of teens and acknowledging how difficult the situation may be.

>> **Example statements:** *"It's frustrating to have to take a pill every day."* **or** *"I can't imagine dealing with all the pressures of using social media."*

Try It Out: Think of a risky behavior your teen has struggled to change. Create an empathizing statement that you could use based on that risky behavior.

Your Statement:

_____

_____

> **Reminder:** Empathizing is not agreement or approval, but it does help to facilitate change.

AVOIDING ARGUMENTS AND ROLLING WITH RESISTANCE – Avoid power struggles to continue open dialogue and exploration of the underlying issue.

>> **Explain your motivations and try not to get defensive. <u>Teen's statement</u>:** *"Everyone else's parents are letting them go, you are ruining my life!"* **<u>Parent's reply</u>:** *"I'm not trying to ruin your life, I'm saying no because I love you and want you to be safe."*

Try It Out: Imagine your teen says *"You're always on my back about school. Leave me alone!"* How could you respond calmly and explain your motivations?

Your Statement:

_____

_____

> **Reminder:** The more we push teens to change, the more resistant they become. Use reflections and open-ended questions to avoid arguments and roll with resistance.

SUPPORTIVE CONFRONTATION – These are similar to amplified reflections and can be most effective when teens are withdrawing and not engaging with you or arguing to sustain a behavior.

>> **Example <u>Teen's statement</u>:** *"Texting and driving is not a problem for anyone except old people."* **<u>Parent's reply</u>:** *"You don't know anything that could happen if you text and drive."*

Try It Out: Imagine your teen says *"Smoking weed isn't a big deal."* Using supportive confrontation, how could you respond?

Your Statement:

_____

_____

PRACTICE: More strategies for handling difficult situations.

EMPHASIZING PERSONAL CONTROL: Admitting to your teen that it's their decision to make, with statements like *"You will make your own decision when faced with this situation...."* or *"You are in control of your body."*

- What concerns do you have, if any, with emphasizing personal control to your teen?

_____

Reminder: It is ultimately the responsibility of all teenagers to make their own behavior changes, and you as the parent have limited control over their decisions once they are out of your sight.

SOCRATIC QUESTIONS:
Questions that when asked, lead teens to present their own arguments for change. Socratic question examples:

- What's the alternative....
- What if.....
- What would it take....

Develop 2 Socratic questions you could use in response to a behavior your teen has been resistant about.

Behavior: _____

Question 1: _____

Question 2: _____

Support Your Teen's SELF-EFFICACY: Help your teen feel confident that change and safer choices are possible, by highlighting their skills and strengths or past successes. Self-efficacy example statements:

- You have used condoms successfully in the past.
- You were able to stay sober at other parties.

Create one statement that is specific to your teen's strengths and or past successes that would support their self-efficacy.

_____

_____

In Summary

Using the Strategies –
Putting It All Into Practice

PARENT PERSPECTIVE: What new strategies will you use first? How will you know if they are working?

_____

_____

_____

> **Reminder:** We have covered a lot of different communication strategies. No one is expecting you to become an expert at every one. Choose the strategies that will work best for you and start with those.

QUICK QUIZ #15: List three elements of non-verbal communication you need to be most aware of when talking with your teen.

1. _____

2. _____

3. _____

Reminder: Two-thirds of all communication is non-verbal! Teens frequently forget what you say or do, but they rarely forget how you make them feel.

Points to Remember

- Parenting is a process and we are growing and learning almost as much as our teens during this time

- Listening is vital – try to facilitate conversations (not lead them)

- Find opportunities for family time (whatever that looks like for your family)

- Find the right time and place for discussions on risky behaviors – someplace where you will have few interruptions and when you are in the right frame of mind

- Help teens think through and voice their reasons and motivations for a behavior

- Help them learn the skills they need to plan for behavior change – brainstorming their own ideas and selecting a path that will work for them

Perhaps most importantly – give yourself a break! If you don't use a strategy entirely correctly, no harm is done. Don't give up; try again next time. The more you practice and try out new strategies, the easier they will become.

QUICK QUIZ #16: Test your *Teen Speak* - True or False

Here are a few questions about the key "takeaways" from the book.

Answer "true" or "false" to each statement, and test your *Teen Speak* knowledge!

1. As a parent, I am learning almost as much as my teen as I work to build a strong relationship with them.

   TRUE   FALSE

2. It is my job to do more of the talking when having discussions with my teen about risky behaviors.

   TRUE   FALSE

3. The "right" kind of family time is eating dinner together every day.

   TRUE   FALSE

4. Asking permission and giving teens an opportunity to suggest a time to talk builds mutual respect between you and your teen.

   TRUE   FALSE

5. When teens think through and voice their reasons and motivations for making safe choices when faced with a risky situation, they are more likely to follow through with their choices.

   TRUE   FALSE

6. When brainstorming with my teen I should provide a variety of options and tell them what they need to do.

   TRUE   FALSE

Answer Sheet

CHAPTER 1:
FOUNDATIONS FOR TALKING WITH YOUR TEEN

QUICK QUIZ #1: List 3 common risky behaviors that contribute to teen deaths.

1. Texting and driving
2. Drinking alcohol
3. Suicide

CHAPTER 2:
TEEN DEVELOPMENT – THE GOOD, THE BAD AND THE BEAUTIFUL

QUICK QUIZ #2: What are the four stages of development that teens will experience during puberty?

1. Physical
2. Emotional
3. Cognitive
4. Sexual

CHAPTER 3:
PHYSICAL DEVELOPMENT – BODY CHANGES

QUICK QUIZ #3: What are some things to watch out for as your teen develops physically?

1. Fear and Withdrawal
2. An obsessive concern about their appearance – causing them to miss school or events because they "didn't look right"
3. Excessive dieting or exercise – which can quickly lead to eating disorders
4. Being bullied, teased, or excluded by friends or other teens

CHAPTER 6:
SEXUAL DEVELOPMENT – CHANGING DESIRES

QUICK QUIZ #4: What are the 6 influencers on a teen's decisions about sex?

1. Personal readiness
2. Family standards
3. Past exposure to sexual abuse
4. Peer pressure
5. Religious values
6. Having the opportunity

CHAPTER 7:
TEENS AND RISKY BEHAVIORS – WHAT ARE THEY DOING?

QUICK QUIZ #5: What is the first and most important step in reducing your teen's risk?

- Start the conversation

CHAPTER 8:
CHANGING BEHAVIORS

QUICK QUIZ #6: What are 2 factors that play the biggest role in your teen's decision making?

1. Perception of risk
2. Intent to take part in a behavior

QUICK QUIZ #7: What is the greatest indicator that a teen will be successful in changing their behavior or in making safer choices?

- Self-efficacy

CHAPTER 11:
BUILDING A STRONG FOUNDATION

QUICK QUIZ #8: Building a strong foundation starts with ASKING PERMISSION. What are 2 benefits to asking your teen permission, before jumping into a discussion with them?

1. Gives your teen some control
2. Your teen pays more attention

PRACTICE: ASKING PERMISSION. Let's say you want to talk to your teen about their friends. You could ask permission like: *"Can we talk about Jamie?"*

What are 2 more ways you could ask permission to talk to your teen about their friends?

1. *"When is a good time to talk about what happened with Jamie?"*
2. *"I would like to talk with you about Jamie, is that OK?"*

What are some ways to respond if your teen says "no"?

- *"This is something we need to talk about. If now is not a good time, what would work better for you?"*
- *"I know I don't have all of the information. I would like to hear your thoughts on what happened with Jamie."*

QUICK QUIZ #9: Building a strong foundation continues with how we GIVE INFORMATION. What are 3 key things to remember when giving information to teens?

1. Make it brief
2. Don't exaggerate the information for effect
3. Be factual

PRACTICE: Building a strong foundation includes OFFERING CONCERN. Give two example statements on how you could offer concern if you found out your teen was in an unhealthy relationship with a friend.

1. *"I'm really worried that you aren't hanging out with anyone except for Jamie anymore."*
2. *"I'm concerned you may be compromising some of the things you like to do just to please Jamie."*

PRACTICE: Building a strong foundation includes providing a MENU OF OPTIONS. When your teen is ready to problem solve or change a behavior, you can offer a menu of options. What are 3 possible options you could offer your teen to avoid unhealthy relationships.

1. *"Think about what a good friend looks like to you. How does Jamie fit that image?"*
2. *"What if you and Jamie both invited some friends to the game and you went as a group."*
3. *"What do you think about spending time with friends without Jamie?"*

CHAPTER 12:
OPEN-ENDED QUESTIONS - LEARNING MORE FROM YOUR TEEN

Circle all of the open-ended questions below:

1. Did you have a good day at school?
2. Do you have homework?
3. (How important is college to you?)
4. Are you hanging out with your friends tomorrow after school?
5. (What would it take for you to feel less stressed?)
6. (When do you see yourself having sex?)

QUICK QUIZ #10: What are some of the issues with using questions that start with *"Why"*?

- They can have unintended overtones of criticism.
- Why questions can be difficult to answer.

PRACTICE: FULLY OPEN QUESTIONS can help you learn more from your teen with less questioning by you. Using the fully open question starters below, insert behaviors or situations you would like to discuss with your teen.

- *Tell me about "what is stressing you out."*
- *What do you think about "drinking at parties?"*
- *How do you decide when to "wear a helmet when you are riding your bike?"*
- *How do you feel about "texting and driving?"*
- *Help me understand "what is going on in school?"*

PRACTICE: KEY QUESTIONS move the focus of the discussion to making a change – and ultimately to making a commitment to change or not engage in a risky behavior. What are some examples of key questions you could use with your teen?

- *"What do you think about putting your phone in the glove box or putting it on 'do not disturb' when you get in the car?"*
- *"What would it take for you to pass your next math test?"*

CHAPTER 13:
AFFIRMATIONS – FOCUSING ON THE POSITIVES

PRACTICE: Using the statement starters below, develop two affirmations for each starter that are specific to your teen.

- *You have....*
  - *"the ability to get good grades in school."*
  - *"high standards for your health."*
- *You are....*
  - *"committed to being safe when you get your driver's license."*
  - *"a good role model for your younger sister."*
- *You feel....*
  - *"it's important to wait to have sex."*
  - *"passionate about getting into college."*
- *You believe....*
  - *"it's important to make your own decisions."*
  - *"you can avoid drinking at parties."*

CHAPTER 14:
REFLECTIONS – LISTENING AND RESPONDING

PRACTICE: Create a response in your own words for each type of reflection below based on this example: *Your teen is struggling to get good grades in school.*

- REPEAT: Repeat back the actual words or repeat an element of what your teen said.
  - *Your reflection:*
    "You're having a hard time getting good grades."
- REPHRASE: Reflect back in your own words the meaning of what they have told you.
  - *Your reflection:*
    "You are working hard and not getting the results you want."

- PARAPHRASE: Make a guess at the meaning of what your teen has said.
  - *Your reflection:*
    "You want to figure out how to improve your grades."
- REFLECTING FEELING: Confirm your understanding of their feelings.
  - *Your reflection:*
    "You're frustrated with failing classes."

CHAPTER 15:
LET THEM TELL YOU WHAT YOU WANT TO HEAR

QUICK QUIZ #11: What does the acronym DARN stand for related to Change Talk?

Desires

Abilities

Reasons

Needs

QUICK QUIZ #12: Circle each statement that is CHANGE TALK:

1. I heard the patch can help you stop smoking.
2. (I need to wear my seatbelt.)
3. I have no issues with my friends.
4. (I want to do better in school.)
5. (I can stop using if I wanted to.)

CHAPTER 16:
PLANNING FOR SUCCESS

PRACTICE: What open-ended questions can you use to help your teen brainstorm ideas for safer decisions when faced with risky situations?

- What do you think you can do?
- What have you heard that other teens have done?

- What if you were to (insert solution to change unhealthy behavior) what would it take?
- Can I share some ideas?

CHAPTER 17:
HANDLING DIFFICULT SITUATIONS - INTRODUCTION

QUICK QUIZ #13: What are the first 2 steps in overcoming difficult behaviors in teens?

- Step 1: Recognize the interpersonal tension – what exactly are they saying to you and how are they saying it?
- Step 2: Monitor your own behavior and take a figurative step back.

CHAPTERS 18 AND 19:
HANDLING DIFFICULT SITUATIONS - STRATEGIES

SIMPLE REFLECTION: Repeating what your teen has said to you in a neutral tone.

- **Teen Statement:** *"I hate going to school every day!"*
- **Your Simple Reflection:**
  "You don't like school"

OMISSION REFELCTION- Reflect the message their behavior is sending.

- **Teen's Behavior:** *Teen is saying nothing while you are trying to talk to them about safe sex. They just keep looking at their phone.*
- **Your Omission Reflection:**
  "You're not comfortable talking about sex with me"

AMPLIFIED REFLECTION- Reflecting what your teen has said in an exaggerated way with empathy and no sarcasm.

- **Teen Statement:** *"I don't need this stupid depression medication!"*
- **Your Amplified Reflection:**
  "You're not feeling depressed any more"

QUICK QUIZ #14: What does the acronym DEARS stand for related to responding to difficult situations?

Developing discrepancies

Empathy

Avoiding arguments

Rolling with resistance

Supportive confrontation

IN SUMMARY:
USING THE STRATEGIES – PUTTING IT ALL INTO PRACTICE

QUICK QUIZ #15: List three elements of non-verbal communication you need to be most aware of when talking with your teen:

1. Eye contact
2. Facial expressions
3. Gestures
4. Tone of voice
5. Pitch
6. Rate of speech
7. Speaking style

QUICK QUIZ #16: Test your *Teen Speak* - True or False

We have covered a lot of different communication strategies. No one is expecting you to become an expert at every one. Choose the strategies that will work best for you and start with those. Here are a few questions about the key "takeaways" from the book.

Answer "true" or "false" to each statement, and test your Teen Speak knowledge!

1. *As a parent, I am learning almost as much as my teen as I work to build a strong relationship with them.*

(TRUE) FALSE

2. It is my job to do more of the talking when having discussions with my teen about risky behaviors.

   TRUE (FALSE)

3. The "right" kind of family time is eating dinner together every day.

   TRUE (FALSE)

4. Asking permission and giving teens an opportunity to suggest a time to talk builds mutual respect between you and your teen.

   (TRUE) FALSE

5. When teens think through and voice their reasons and motivations for making safe choices when faced with a risky situation, they are more likely to follow through with this choice.

   (TRUE) FALSE

6. When brainstorming with my teen I should provide a variety of options and tell them what they need to do.

   TRUE (FALSE)

Made in the USA
Columbia, SC
30 September 2019